PROPHETS

Distinctions Between Real and False Prophets
Part I

CHARLES CHIBWE

Ottawa, Canada, 2024

Published by:

AFROCA IN CANADA PRESS (ACP)

Ottawa, Ontario, Canada

www.acpress.ca

ISBN: 978-1-988251-22-6

DEDICATION

For my family:

My wife,

Abigail:

And our three lovely children,

Zachariah, Cynthia & Destiny.

CONTENTS

ACKNOWLEDGMENTS

I am deeply indebted to my wife, Abigail Chibwe, who has been instrumental in providing logistical and emotional support.

In the similar vein, I am grateful to my daughter, Cynthia, for providing stationery materials and other supports that have been helpful in the preparation of this book.

My sincere gratitude goes to my ex-brother-in-law, Kelvin Mulemi. Mr. Mulemi provided the laptop which I used to brainstorm on the content of this book.

I wish also to acknowledge Pastor Pax Lukenda Chola of the Royal Family Ministries for providing some useful scriptural information on some topics covered in this book.

My acknowledgement, too, goes to Professor Charles David Mwewa of Canada. He has really made my dream of being a published author come true. He provided all the copy editing, editorial and structuring and sponsored the publication of this book in totality.

I am deeply indebted to the members of the New Heaven Church Ministries for their diligence in Church attendance, Sunday after Sunday. Without them, I would not have had the inspiration necessary to pen this book.

Last, but not least, my sincere gratitude goes to City University of Science and Technology

Management Precem campus in Kabangwe, where we meet for Church service every Sunday. They truly provide a home for the congregation.

PREFACE

Pastor Charles Chibwe and I share many things in common. We are blood brothers. We love the Word of God and our Lord Jesus Christ. We are ordained Gospel Ministers. We love to pray. We have three children each. There are also many other similarities, an additional one being that we love to read and write.

Around 1990/91, Pastor Chibwe came to Kapisha, a small shanty compound in Chingola, Zambia and took me to Lusaka, Zambia's Capital City. At that time, that was my greatest dream: to visit Lusaka. I remember vividly as we walked along Lumumba Road *en route* to Emmasdale, where my late cousin lived.

This trip changed everything. In Acts 11:21-23, there is a story of Barnabas: "The hand of the Lord was with them, and a great number of people believed and turned to the Lord. When news of this reached the ears of the church in Jerusalem, they sent Barnabas to Antioch. When he arrived and saw the grace of God, he rejoiced and encouraged them all to abide in the Lord with all their hearts."

That little passage above, perfectly describes the ministry of Pastor Chibwe. He is a quintessential encourager. I reside in Canada, and I miss my family (mother, brothers and sisters) in Zambia. But Pastor Chibwe has lessened this pain by always being there to update me about my family's welfare in Zambia.

And on Facebook, Pastor Chibwe is my number one fan: always providing encouraging feedback and comments. Pastor Chibwe is selfless, great in good deed, and a sympathetic leader and family man.

Pastor Chibwe has generally been concerned about the infiltration of false "prophets" into the Church whose motive is it to rob God of His glory. These so-called prophets come in the sheep's clothes but inside, they are full of greed, self-love and deceit. In this book, Rev. Chibwe, in no uncertain way, makes a clear distinction between true and false prophets. It is a clarion call to be vigilant and to be on the watch against spiritual masqueraders. Pastor Chibwe re-echoes the call of His Lord who warned that in the Last Days, "…many false prophets will arise and mislead many. Because of the multiplication of wickedness, the love of most will grow cold" (Matthew 24:11-12).

The Lord didn't say, "Probably or may be," His warning was unequivocal: "…many false prophets will rise…." This book should serve as a follow-up to that warning and as a reminder that the Church should be careful not to entertain God's enemies who rise in the name of God.

I warmly and gladly recommend this book as ready tool for the Church to both read and use in its devotions.

Charles Mwewa
Author and Publisher,
Canada, 2024

1 | DEFINING A PROPHET

A prophet is God's spokesperson. He or she is a divinely called minister who announces the will of God to the people. Such a person can be called a real prophet. True prophets hear from God and convey what they hear from God to the people. The duty of a prophet, therefore, is to prophesy or utter prophesies (prophetic utterances). They may utter prophesies to predict the future, and they may report to the people what God is doing in the present.

In Isaiah 38:5, we read, "Go and tell Hezekiah, this is what the LORD, the God of your Father David, says: I have heard your prayer and seen your tears: I will add fifteen years to your life" (NIV). It was the recovery of Hezekiah that the LORD conveyed the message through Prophet Isaiah. The prophet is the mouthpiece of God. To prophesy is to bring the exact result that God intended. And this verse illustrates this definition of a prophecy. If the prophecy is for healing, healing should take place. If for deliverance, deliverance should take place. Prophecy is to theology what equations are to arithmetic: They both involve the balancing of numbers. Where there is prophecy, there must be the fulfillment. True prophecy brings the equilibrium to God's interests. It fulfills God's purposes on earth.

In Jeremiah 28:9, we read, "The prophet which prophesieth of peace, when the word of the prophet shall come to pass, then shall the prophet be known, that the LORD hath truly sent him" (KJV). And in Mathew 26:68, we read, "Saying, Prophesy unto us, thou Christ, who is he that smote thee?" (KJV) Thus, Jeremiah can be rendered as, "The prophet who expounds, teaches, and preaches the truth, when the Word comes to pass then shall that prophet be known that the Lord has truly sent him." While Mathew may be rendered as, "Tell us you Christ Jesus who smote thee?" Therefore, as stated earlier, the other meaning of prophesying is to teach, preach and expound the Word of God.

In Israel, under the dispensation of the law, Kings and prophets prophesized. They spoke prophetic utterances.1 Samuel 28:6, "And when Saul inquired of the LORD, the LORD answered him not, neither by dreams, nor by Urim, nor by prophets" (KJV). This happened when King Saul disobeyed God. Prophet Samuel told King Saul to go and fight the Amalekites and that he should not spare anything pertaining to the Amalekites. King Saul destroyed everything of the Amalekites. However, King Saul spared Agag the Amalekites' king. He also spared the fatted cows, rams and oxen so that when he returned from battle, he would sacrifice the fatted tamed animals and Agag would be beheaded. Saul went against the will of God. The Lord commanded him to destroy all, not to spare some.

It was not the duty of the king in Israel to perform sacrifices, those were duties for priests. In 1 Samuel 15:22-23, we read, "And Samuel said, Hath the LORD as great delight in burnt offerings and sacrifices, as in obeying the voice of the LORD? Behold, to obey is better than sacrifice, and to hearken than the fat of rams. For rebellion is as the sin of witchcraft, and stubbornness is as iniquity and idolatry. Because thou hast rejected the word of the LORD, he hath also rejected thee from being king" (KJV). Before King Saul's disobedience, God could come to him through dreams and prophets, and King Saul spoke prophetic utterances. After disobedience, he could not.

David was a great king and a man after God's own heart, and at the same time, a prophet. King David spoke prophetic utterances. Psalms 22:16-18, we read, "For dogs have compassed me: the assembly of the wicked have enclosed me: they pierced my hands and my feet. I may tell all my bones: they look and stare upon me. They part my garments among them, and cast lots upon my vesture" (KJV). And in

Mark 15:24, we read, "And when they had crucified him, they parted his garments, casting lots upon them, what every man should take" (KJV).

One thousand years prior, David had prophesized of the death of Jesus Christ before his birth. David was born around 1000 BC and Jesus was born around 6 AD. In the Old Testament Israel, Kings were used by God to prophesy and speak God's Rhema (the now word). However, they did not preach and teach the Word of God. Preaching and teaching were left solely in the hands of prophets, priests and the elders of the congregations. Besides ruling the kingdom of Israel and uttering prophetic utterances, Kings went out and fought in battles.

Some Old Testament Prophets

Moses was a great prophet who ever lived on earth. It is written in Deuteronomy 34:10, "And there arose not a prophet since in Israel like unto Moses, whom the LORD knew face to face" (KJV). God confronted Miriam, the prophetess and older sister to Moses. He told her that He could only speak to her through visions and dreams but to His servant Moses, it was face to face. Moses prophesized of the coming of Jesus Christ as the great prophet: "I will raise them up a Prophet from among their brethren, like unto thee, and will put my words in his mouth: and he shall speak unto them all that I shall command him," (Deuteronomy 18:18, KJV).

Moslems argue that Moses did not prophesy of the coming of Jesus as a great prophet. They opine that the one Moses talked about was Muhammad. They cite in Deuteronomy 33:1-3 and Habakkuk 3:3, where God talked about the prophesies on three mountains: Sinai, Zion and Paran. Moslems believe that it is a well-known fact that the prophecy of Sinai was given to Prophet Moses and that the prophecy of Zion, for Bethlehem of Judah, was given in respect of Jesus:

> And the LORD spake unto me, saying, Ye have compassed this mountain long enough: turn you northward. And command thou the people, saying, Ye are to pass through the coast of your brethren the children of Esau, which dwell in Seir: and they shall be afraid of you: take ye good heed unto yourselves therefore: Meddle not with them: for I will not give you of their land, no, not so much as a foot breadth: because I have given mount Seir unto Esau for a possession. Ye shall buy meat of them for money, that ye may eat and ye shall also buy water of them for money, that ye may drink. For the LORD thy God hath blessed thee in all the works of thy hand: he knoweth thy walking through this great wilderness: these forty years the LORD thy God hath been with thee: thou hast lacked nothing. And when we passed by from our brethren the children of Esau, which dwelt in Seir, through the way of the plain from Elath, and from Eziongaber, we turned and passed by the way of the wilderness of Moab. And the LORD said unto me, Distress not the Moabites, neither contend with them in battle:

> for I will not give thee of their land for a possession: because I have given Ar unto the children of Lot for a possession. The Emims dwelt therein in times past, a people great, and many, and tall, as the Anakims…. (Deuteronomy 2:2-10, KJV).

Therefore, Moslems believe that the prophecy of Mount Paran, without any doubt, was given to Granel, the son of Ismael – because they were the inhabitants of that particular place as it is mentioned in the Bible:

> God heard the boy crying, and the angel of God called to Hagar from heaven and said to her, "What is the matter, Hagar? Do not be afraid: God has heard the boy crying as he lies there. Lift the boy up and take him by the hand, for I will make him into a great nation." Then God opened her eyes and she saw a well of water. So, she went and filled the skin with water and gave the boy a drink. God was with the boy as he grew up. He lived in the desert and became an archer. While he was living in the Desert of Paran, his mother got a wife for him from Egypt (Genesis 21:17-21).

Moslems believe that this was Prophet Muhammad (or Mohammed) who came from Kedar, one of the sons of Ismael (Genesis 25:13). The one who was like unto Moses, Islam believes, was Mohammed and not Jesus.

This is a false belief. Islam believes that Ismael lived in the wilderness of Paran and when Moses prophesized of a prophet unto him to come it was definitely Mohammed. They conclude this because the prophecy was made in the wilderness of Paran. What Islam forgets, however, is that the Nation of Israel was a promise God gave to Abraham and Sarah and not to Hagar. Jesus Christ is the only seed to come – He is the Seed of Abraham. As it is written in Galatians 3:19, "Wherefore then serveth the law? It was added because of transgression, till the seed should come to whom the promise was made, it was ordained by angels in the hand of a mediator."

Eli was a High Priest, judge and prophet of Israel.

Nathan was the prophet of Israel, who confronted David when David committed adultery with Bathsheba, Uriah's wife. David eliminated Uriah by telling Joab to put him in the battle-front and retire him so that he was killed.

Elijah was a prophet of fire, the light of Israel, a judgmental prophet who killed 450 prophets of Balim. He commanded fire from heaven that killed 102 armies of Ahab at Mount Carmel. Elijah wiped out idolatries in Israel. He challenged Israel to make a choice and ascertain how long they would live with two opinions. That if God be their God, they should serve Him and if Baal be their god, they should serve him.

Both Elisha and Elijah were the lights of Israel who oversaw Israel. Elisha received double portions of anointing from God through obeying Elijah. He also presided over the chariot and fire of Israel (2

Kings 13:14). Now, Elisha had fallen sick of his sickness "wherefore he died." And Joash the King of Israel came down unto him and wept over his face and said, "O my Father, my Father! The chariot of Israel and the horsemen thereof."

Major prophets were Isaiah, Jeremiah, Ezekiel and Daniel. They prophesized of near and distance futures and their prophecies were longer than those of the minor prophets. Isaiah had an eagle's eye: God could use him to see what was happening in Israel and around the globe. He was also called the Evangelist of the Old Testament. Most of his prophecies talked much about the coming of Jesus Christ and His works. In

Isaiah 7:14, we read, "Therefore the Lord himself shall give you a sign: Behold a virgin shall conceive and bring forth a son and they shall call his name Immanuel." This is repeated in Mathew1:23, "Behold, a virgin shall be with a child, and bring forth a son and they shall call his name Immanuel, which being interpreted is, God with us."

In Isaiah 61:1, we read, "The spirit of the Lord is upon me: because the Lord hath anointed me to preach good tidings unto the meek: he hath sent me to bind the broken hearted, to preach liberty to the captives and the opening of the prison to them that are bound." This is, thus, repeated in Luke 4:18-19, "The spirit of the Lord is upon me because he hath anointed me to preach the gospel to the poor: he hath sent me to heal the broken hearted, to preach deliverance to the captives and recovering of the sight to the blind: to set at liberty to them that are bruised: to preach acceptable year of the Lord.

Isaiah's book is called the Fifth Gospel.

Daniel and Ezekiel were prophets who went into captivity in Babylon. Daniel served into dynasties, Babylonian and Persia-Medes. Daniel was devoted to the life of prayer whilst in exile. He prayed three times a day facing South-west, towards Jerusalem and the Temple. Most of his prophecies point to the four kingdoms that would conquer the world: Babylon, Persia-Medes, Greece and Rome. He prophesized of the visions of the seventy weeks of the increase of knowledge, of the technological world and the Internet Age, of the global world in which we are now.

Ezekiel prophesized to Israel as a whole, especially to those who were in slavery.

Jeremiah was known as the Weeping Prophet: he warned Judah that if they did not repent, they would be slaves in a foreign land and would be there for seventy years (see Jeremiah 29:10: Jeremiah 25:11-13).

Minor Prophets

Their prophecies were for the immediate or contemporary future and they did not prophesy for a longer period of time. They include Amos, Habakkuk, Hagai, Hosea, Joel, and Jonah. Others are Malachi,

Micah, Nahum, Obadiah, Zechariah, Zephaniah and John the Baptist.

John the Baptist was the forerunner of the Messiah, the voice that cried in the wilderness and the least among all the prophets, and ironically, he was the greatest of all.

Prophets in the New Testament or Church Dispensation

John the Apostle was the prophet in the Church Age. The youngest amongst the disciples of Jesus, he was also called the Son of Thunder, because of his dedication and prayer life. John, the revelator, lived longer amongst the apostles of Jesus Christ. He died at the age of 98 at the Island of Patmos in Ephesus where he was imprisoned. He was the one who wrote the Gospel of Saint John, First, Second and Third John and the Book of Revelation.

Agabus was the prophet of the Church in Antioch. All believers were called Christians for the first time in Antioch (Acts 11:26). The Church in Antioch had all it takes for the perfection of the saints: it had apostles, prophets, teachers, evangelists and pastors. These five are collectively known as the Five-fold Ministers. A healthy Church is a Church that has the five-fold ministries. Sometimes God gives the five-fold ministries in an individual and this happened mostly in the pioneering stage of the Church. Sometimes God can give you one ministerial office and add some spiritual gifts to it. Him alone God is the one who calls people to work in His kingdom.

In 1 Corinthians 12:1, we read, "Now, dear brothers and sisters, regarding your question about the special abilities the Spirit gives us. I don't want you to misunderstand this" (NLT). And in 1 Corinthians 12:11, we read, "It is the one and only Spirit who distributes all these gifts. He alone decides which gift each person should have" (NLT). It is one Spirit who works in all believers. God is the only one who can call and give you the ministerial offices as well as adding some spiritual gifts, like healings, workers of miracles, and so on.

Even today in this dispensation of the Church, God has the ability to raise prophets who can do His will. According to John 14:12, "Verily, verily, I say unto you, He that believeth on me, the works that I do shall he do also: and greater works than these shall he do: because I go unto my Father" (KJV). It is evident that God can raise prophets who can do greater things as long as they have faith in God.

2 | ACCURACY OF PROPHESY

The Test of Accuracy

A real prophet of God must prophesy with accuracy. A real prophet of God Almighty must speak prophetic utterances in sincerity and in truth. When he speaks prophetic utterances, it must happen exactly. Remember what he uttered some time may not happened just there but it will happen in future exactly the way he spoke about it.

The prophetic utterance must command an overview of every thing and when fulfillment comes it must be exactly.

Panorama of a prophetic utterance: It is a complete survey of a subject, a complete series of events. This is what we call real accuracy of a prophecy. It is where a prophet tells you that, "Tomorrow you will receive a brand-new blue Toyota

Corolla at 14:30 hrs.," and the receiver receives exactly prophesized. This prophecy is real and accurate.

When a prophet prophesizes to you that, "I see a Toyota Corolla coming to you," and you need to ask the so-called prophet, when will I receive it? And what colour shall be that Toyota Corolla? If he does not prophesy of a complete series of event then it is not a real prophecy

Isaiah prophesized that God would raise Cyrus, a Persian king, to allow Israel to go back to their home land from slavery and to go and rebuild the Temple of Jerusalem (Isaiah 44:28). This prophecy is real and accurate because Isaiah prophesized that the name of the Persian king would be Cyrus before even Cyrus was born. It took one hundred and fifty years when the prophecy was fulfilled.

In 2 Kings 4:15-17, we read, "And he said, call her and when he called her, she stood in the door, and he said, about this season, according to the time of life, thou shall embrace a son. And she said, nay my Lord, thou man of God, don't lie unto thine handmaid. The woman conceived and bore a son at the season that Elisha had said unto her according to the time of life."

The Shunamite woman was barren, the same woman built an upper room for Elisha to live in. She was a woman of hospitality yet barren. When she was called to stand on the door of the upper chamber, Elisha prophesized to her that about that time according to the time of life she would embrace a son. It happened the same as Elisha prophesized to her, she had a baby after a year. Verse seventeen of second Kings says the woman conceived and bore a son at the season that Elisha had said according to the time of life. It was an accurate prophecy: it happened exactly as he prophesized – the woman embraced the baby the following year, same time as he had said.

In Gen. 18:9-15 we read:

> And they said unto him, where is Sarah thy wife? And he said, behold in the tent. And they said, I will certainly return unto thee according to the time of life: and lo Sarah thy wife shall have a son and Sarah heard it in the tent door, which was behind her. Now Sarah and Abraham were old and well stricken in age: And it ceased to be with Sarah after the manner of women. Therefore, Sarah laughed within herself saying after I am waxed old also? And the Lord said unto Abraham, wherefore did Sarah laugh saying, shall I of a surety bear a son, which I am old? Is any thing too hard for the Lord? At the time appointed will return to thee, according to the time of life and Sarah shall have a son. Then Sarah denied saying, I laugh not: for she was afraid and she said, nay: thou didst laugh.

When angels of the Lord visited Abraham and his wife Sarah, an angel came to fulfill the prophecy through which God promised them that they would never go childless. Sarah, within herself, laughed and doubted because of her age!

Both Sarah and the woman of Shumen were very old, they had already reached the stage were where they cannot have children any more. Is any thing too hard for the Lord, for with God nothing shall be impossible?

Both Sarah and the Shunammite woman received their prophecies on the doors. The angel told Sarah that he would certainly return unto her according to the time of life. That meant within the same season as he had spoken to Sarah, the same season the following year she bore a son. The prophecy was accurate.

Another accurate prophecy to consider is the one concerning Elijah. In James 5:17-18, we read that, "Elias was a man subject to passion as we are and he prayed earnestly that it might not rain: And it did not rain by a space of three years and six months. And he prayed again and the heaven gave rain and the earth brought forth fruit."

Again, in 1 Kings 17:1, we read, "And Elijah the Tishbite, who was the inhabitant of Gilead, said unto Ahab, as the Lord God of Israel liveth, before whom I stand, there shall not be dew nor rain these years, but according to my word."

The writer of the book of Kings didn't mention of the years when the draught would last but he said there would not be dew or rain for the coming years. James says it would not rain for three years and half. The prophetic prayer of Elijah was more on the rains, the fact that it did not rain as he prophesized about and it did not rain for three and half years as James put it. It shows correctly that it was an accurate prophecy.

Why Elijah prophesized that it would not rain? It was due to the evil that Ahab and Jezebel had brought in Israel of worshiping idols. Israel was occupied by strange gods: the worship of Balim and false prophets. Ahab and his wife Jezebel were there to eliminate the prophets of God Almighty: "For it was so, when Jezebel cut off the prophets of the Lord, that Obediah took a hundred prophets and hid them by fifty in cave" (1 Kings 18:4).

But in 2 Kings 7:1-2, "Then Elisha said, hear ye the word of the Lord: Thus, saith the Lord, tomorrow about this time shall a measure of flour be sold for a shekel, and two measures of barley for a shekel: in the gate of Samaria. Then the Lord on whose hand the king learned answered the man of God and said, behold, if the Lord would make windows in heaven, might this thing be? And he said behold thou shall see it with thine eyes, but shall not eat thereof."

There was famine in the days of prophet Elisha. The prophet prophesized that the following day about that time would a measure of flour be sold a dollar in the gate of Samaria. The economist whom the king trusted so much refused to believe that would happen for the drought was grievous. The economist challenged Elisha that even though God was to open windows in heaven, hunger could not finish in Israel.

People used to eat their fellow human being as meat for food. Prophet Elisha told the economist to believe him, and the economist would see it with his naked eyes but, unfortunately, the economist would not feast on it. Elisha's prophesy was filled in 2 Kings 7:18-20. It was accurate.

In 1 Kings 17:11-15, we read:

> And as she was going to fetch it [water], he called to her and said, bring me ,I pray thee a morsel of bread in thine hand, and she said as the Lord thy God liveth, I have not a cake but hand full of meal in a barrel and little of oil in a cruise: behold, I am gathering two sticks that I may go in and dress it for me and my son, that we may eat and die. And Elijah said to her fear not and do as thou hast said: But make me therefore a little cake first and bring it unto me and after making for thee and thy and for and for thy son. For thus saith the Lord God of Israel, the barrel of meal shall not waste, neither shall cruse of oil fail until the day of the Lord sendeth rain upon the earth. She went and did according to the saying of Elisha: And she and her house did eat many days.

Elijah ushered in a prophetic word of utterance to the widow of Zarephath: "and Elijah said to her fear not and do as thou hast said: but make me therefore little cake first and bring it unto me and after make for thee and for thy son, for thus saith the Lord God of Israel, the barrel meal shall not waste, neither shall cruise of oil fail until the day when the Lord sends rain upon the earth."

The widow went and did according to what the prophet said. She heard that prophetic word from the man of God and acted accordingly. The widow had the last meal and little oil to bake the last meal, there and then the following day, they would die. She obeyed a prophetic word of utterance of the man of God and the miracles started happening. Every day a barrel of meal was full and the cruise of oil was full. The woman did not lack food in her home until the drought was finished on earth. The prophetic word that the man of God spoke was accurate and had fulfilled the will of God.

Another lesson to be told from the scriptures is, thus, hearing the Word of God and doing it command bigger blessings. A man of God deserves the first help for he prays for the people in Church and the world as a whole.

A Real Prophecy Comes to Pass

Joel 2:28 says: "And it shall come to pass afterward I will pour out my Spirit upon all flesh: and your sons and daughters shall prophesy and your old men shall dream dreams, young men shall see visions."

Acts 2:16-17 says: "But this is which was spoken by the prophet Joel: And it shall come to pass in the last days saith God, I will pour out my spirit upon all flesh: and your sons and daughters shall prophesy and your young men shall see vision and your old men shall dream dreams."

Some prophecies cannot be fulfilled just there, some may take days, weeks, months, and some years to be fulfilled. Joel prophesized some years ago for this prophecy to be fulfilled on the Day of Pentecost. Believers received the gifts of the Holy Spirit on the Day of Pentecost. It is now over two thousand years ago when the outpouring of the Holy Ghost was fulfilled. Many people have been, and are being, baptized with the Holy Ghost and fire.

Mathew 3:11 says: "I indeed baptize you with water unto repentance: but he that cometh after me is mightier that I whose shoes I am not worthy to bear: He shall baptize you with the Holy Ghost and with fire."

A Real Prophet Must Know and Understand the Fulfillment of Scriptures

Luke 24:44 says: "And he said unto them, these are the word which I spake unto you, while I was yet with you, that all things must be fulfilled, which were written in the law of Moses and in the prophets and in the psalms concerning me."

All the Old Testament scriptures were pointing to Jesus. The centre of every prophecy was Jesus and is he even now. A real prophet must study the scriptures and evaluate them whether they have been fulfilled or not. A prophet must be a student of scriptures. Paul told Timothy to study to show himself approved unto God, a workman that needed not to be ashamed, rightly dividing the Word of Truth. It was or it is by the inspiration of God, that prophets should prophesy, preach, or teach the Word of God. God is the only one to depend upon. By inspiration, it means God breathed, God revealing truths to the prophets. God has been revealing truth and he has continued to inspire his chosen people through the Holy Spirit.

1 Cor. 13:12 reads, "For now we see through a glass, darkly: but then face to face. Now I know in part but then shall I know even as also I am known."

Isaiah 28:10 reads, "Precept must be upon precept, precept upon precept: line upon line, here little and there little."

A Real Prophet Must Know Biblical Doctrines

In 2 Timothy16-17, we read, "All scripture is given by inspiration of God and is profitable for doctrine, for reproof, for correction, for instruction in righteousness: That the man of God may be perfect, thoroughly furnished into all good works." Biblical doctrine is the doctrine that teaches that there is only one God.

Isaiah 44:6 reads, "Thus said the Lord the king of Israel and his redeemer the Lord of hosts: I am the first and the last: and besides me there is no God."

Deut. 6:4 reads, "Hear, O Israel the Lord our God is one Lord." As you worship and pray to God you must remember that there are no three Gods in personalities. There is only one God in person. On the contrary, most people ask: Who is Jesus? Is he the Son of God or is he God the Son? We refer to John 3:16: "For God so love the world that he gave his only begotten son, that whosoever believe in him should not perish but have everlasting life." Jesus is the Son of God one hundred percent. For the Holy Ghost overshadowed Mary and she conceived. God is a Spirit and he is invisible (John 4:24). That child Jesus was born through the will of God but not of the blood, nor the will of the flesh (Jon1:13). God told Moses that Moses could not see him and live. God is invisible, omnipresent, and omnipotent.

If you say he is God the Son (Jesus) then you are affirming that there are two or three personalities of the Godhead: Three persons of God. This will lead to heresy. God is one, the pregnancy that Mary carried was through the Holy Ghost and baby Jesus was born full of the Holy Spirit.

All men in the world were born through the blessing God pronounced to our first parents, Adam and Eve (Gen1:27-28) to be, "fruitful and multiply." No wander every human being who is living here on earth was born through this blessing. But the birth of Jesus is through the Holy Spirit, that is, God himself.

We call Jesus the Son of God but not God the son. The flesh or his body was of a human being and the Spirit which was in him was and is God himself. Philip asked Jesus to show him the Father but Jesus told him that, "I have been so long time with you Philip and he who has seen me [Jesus] has seen the Father and how saying show me the Father?" (John 14:8-9). Jesus is the only begotten of the Father full of truth. All the fullness of the Godhead dwells in Christ Jesus (Col. 2:9).

In John 5:7, we read, "For there are three that bear record in heaven, the Father, the Word and the Holy Ghost and these three are one." When you talk of the Father you talk of God himself. The Word was with the Father who spoke and Jesus came into existence (the Word became flesh and dwelt among us and we beheld his glory, the glory of the only begotten of the Father full of grace and truth). The Holy Spirit is God himself.

The Prophet Must Understand the Language in which the Bible was Originally Written

In order to understand and interpret the Bible correctly, the student of the Bible must be familiar with its various expressions and figures of speech in the Bible. We shall make no attempt to give an exhaustive study of these but rather to just mention some of the more common ones.

A Parable

A parable teaches a spiritual truth by analogy from a natural situation. The word parable implies a placing along side of, for the purpose of comparison. The essential element of the parable is the spiritual lesson to be taught.

A parable is an earthly story with a heavenly meaning. It may or not be a true story. A parable is an extended simile.

Jesus gave us the reason why he taught in parables: "And with many such parables spake he the word unto them as they were able to hear. But without a parable spake he not unto them" (Mark 4:33-34).

There were two reasons why parables were used: (1) To make truth known to the sincere disciples of our Lord, who really did desire to understand God's Word: and (2) to hide the truth from the idly curious, the ones who really did not desire to understand God's Word.

Because of this, we need spiritual wisdom and divine inspiration in the interpretation of a parable. It is important to relate the story to the background of social customs of that time. It is necessary to understand how much of the parable was interpreted by the speaker or by the context. The parable threw light on a doctrine. Remember it was meant to be an illustration of truth. Also, we must be careful that we do not read into parable more than what was meant. We should look for the parable to illustrate one main spiritual truth.

An Allegory

An allegory is sometimes called a prolonged metaphor. It is often involved narration of an artificial event or story in which all the details are determined by the realities they point to and the message they are meant to convey. Thus, in an allegory there need be no attempt to be true to life, whereas the parable always presents a real familiar life situation. One of the most familiar examples of an allegory is Bunyan's *Pilgrim's Progress*. A well-known allegory in the Bible is found in the two sons of Abraham representing two continents (Gal. 4:22-31).

A Type

A Type is divinely appointed illustration of some scriptural truth. A Type is a shadow cast on the pages of the Old Testament history by truth whose full embodiment or anti-type is found in the New Testament revelation.

The English word, "Type," is derived from the Greek word called *Tupos* which occurs sixteen times in the New Testament. The Greek word is very striking and has many shades of meanings. It is translated by such words as, print, figure, pattern, and etc.

Types may be classified as follows:

1. A person, e.g., Adam, Isaac, Jonah, and etc.:
2. An event, e.g., deliverance from Egyptian bondage, the wilderness journey, the conquest of Canaan, and etc.:
3. A thing, e.g., a veil of the Tabernacle, brazen serpent, and etc.:
4. Rituals, e.g., the offerings, the Passover, and etc.

Types have these characteristics:

1. They are thoroughly rooted in history:
2. They are prophetic in nature:
3. They are designed as part of redemptive history:
4. They are centred on Christ: and
5. They have spiritual meaning in both dispensations

A true Type must be:

1. A true picture of the person or thing it prefigures:
2. Of divine appointment: and
3. A picture which prefigures something future.

A study of Types is not easy. It calls for much time, work and prayer. Nevertheless, a study of *typology* is very important for true understanding of God's Word.

A Type must never be used to teach doctrine, but only to illustrate a doctrine which is clearly taught elsewhere.

An Antitype

Certain Old Testament items and practices are called types of New Testament truths. The New Testament realities are the Antitypes. Thus, we can see the relation between types and Antitypes between the Canaan rest and the heavenly rest. Many Old Testament types point forward to Jesus Christ. He is the Antitype of the Tabernacle, its priest and its offering.

A Shadow

You can never have a shadow without a body to cast the shadow. In Old Testament you have the shadow, but in New Testament you meet the body which cast the shadow.

A Simile

A simile is where one thing is likened to another by direct statement. Generally, the words *like* or *as* is used. In Psalm 1:3, we read, "And he shall be *like* a tree planted by the rivers of water…" (emphasis mine). In Prov. 25:25, it is written, "*As* cold waters to a thirsty soul, so is good news from a far country," (emphasis mine). And in 1 Cor. 13:1, we find another simile, "…*as* sounding brass, or a tinkling cymbal" (emphasis mine).

A Metaphor

A metaphor is where one thing is likened to another by implication. Words are taken from their literal meaning and a new and striking use. In Eph 2:20, it is written, "And are built upon the foundation of the apostles and prophets, Jesus Christ himself being the chief corner stone." In Psalm23:1, it is written, "The Lord is my shepherd: I shall not want."

Here is a comparison of these figures of speech:

Metaphor: Isaiah 40:6: flesh is grass
Psalms 100:3: sheep of his pasture

Simile: 1 Peter 1:24: flesh as grass
Isaiah 53:6: we like sheep

A Personification

A Personification is a figure of speech whereby an inanimate object, an object of nature, or abstract idea is given attribute of life. In Numbers 16:32, we read that, "Earth opened her mouth…"

An Apostrophe

This word comes from the Greek meaning to turn. This figure of speech is turning from the readers or hearers and addressing that which is absent as present, or addressing the inanimate as living. Consider 1 Cor. 15:55, "O death, where is thy sting? O grave where is thy victory?"

A Hyperbole

This is a rhetorical figure to magnify an object beyond reality. It is an overstatement used for the purpose of deep emphasis with no thought of deception. Consider John 21:25, "I suppose that even the world itself could not contain the books that should be written."

here.

3 | A SANCTIFIED CHRUCH

Sanctification

Every Church must go under the process of Sanctification. To sanctify is to set apart for God's use. It is the work of the Holy Spirit.

Joel 2:16 says, "Gather the people, sanctify the congregation, assemble the elders, gather children and those who suck the breasts: Let the bridegroom go forth of his chamber and the bride out of her closet.

This is where all ages of inhabitants have come in the Church of the living God with the bridegroom who is Jesus in their midst where sanctification is taking place. It is the people who should surrender to God and sanctify themselves, towards holiness. God the Holy Spirit comes in to sanctify the Church. The entire Church must be sanctified: Elders, leaders, men, women the youths, and children.

Both Aaron and his sons who served in the priestly offices were sanctified. The place of worship, the house where the Almighty God is worshiped, must be holy. In 2 Chronicles 20:13-15, we are reminded that:

> All of Judah stood before the Lord with their little ones, their wives and their children, then upon Jahaziel the son of Benaiah, the son of Jeiel, the son of Mattaniah, a Levite, the son of Asaph, came the Spirit of the Lord in the midst of the congregation. And he said, hearken you all Judah and ye inhabitants of Jerusalem and thou king Jehoshaphat, thus saith the Lord unto you, be not afraid or dismayed by reason of this multitude: for the battle is not yours but God's.

That was the time when Jerusalem-Judah was being attacked by the Moabites, Ammonites and Edomites. These three neighbouring nations teamed up to attack and take away everything in Jerusalem-Judah. The enemies camped in Hazazontamar in Engedi to make sure Jerusalem-Judah was attacked and defeated.

Jehoshaphat feared greatly and set himself to seek the Lord, and proclaimed a fast throughout Jerusalem. The inhabitants of Jerusalem gathered themselves to ask forgiveness from the Almighty God. Jehoshaphat stood in the midst of the congregation of Jerusalem, in the house of the Lord before a new court. A prophetic utterance came from Jahaziel, the son of Zachariah, the son of Benaiah, the son of Jeiel, the son of Mattaniah, a Levite, the son of

Asaph and said demanded that they all hearken to the voice of the Lord, and not to be afraid.

A Church is a place where the saints seek the Lord in truth and in spirit, and are sanctified. Here they are washed in the blood of Jesus, and dedicate themselves before God. When they gather in the will of God, a prophetic utterance may come. Here the people sanctify themselves before God. Without the sanctification of members in the Church, it would be a dry assembly.

Agabus was a prophet in the Church t Antioch. It was at Antioch where they first called believers as Christians. The Church at Antioch was led by the Spirit of God, perfection the saints in the Church. Prophetic utterances were common among the saints in the Church. A prophetic utterance is a voice of one saint or believer through whom God has spoken to the Church or an assembly. Usually, the word that comes through the prophet are the words of encouragement, edification and exaltations.

The early Church was sanctified. Peter prophesied to Ananias and Saphira. Consider Acts 5:1-5:

> But a certain man named Ananias with his wife Saphira, sold a possession and kept back part of the price, his wife also being privy to it, and brought a certain part and let it at the apostles' feet. But Peter said, Ananias, why hath Satan filled thine heart to lie to the Holy Ghost and to keep part of the price of the land? Whiles it remained, was it not thine own? And after it was sold, was it not in thine own power? Why

> hath thou conceived this thing in thine heart? Thou hath not lied unto me but unto God. And Ananias hearing these words fell down and gave up the ghost: and a great fear came on all of them that heard these things.

In the midst of the assembly, Peter spoke a prophetic word of judgment. It was judgmental because it confronted Ananias and Saphira of lying to the Holy Ghost by keeping part of the money they received from selling the property. Before they sold it, it was their property and after they sold it, the money was for them. Why then did they do such a foolish thing? They did not lie to men but to God. Ananias and his wife wowed to give all the money to God. They were supposed to report and speak the truth to the apostles. But they lied and met with judgment. The truth always sets free.

In Acts 2:42-43, we read that, "And they continued steadfastly in the apostles' doctrine and fellowship and in breaking of bread and in prayers and fear come upon every soul; and many wonders and signs were done by the apostles." A great move of God swept across the early Church because they continued in the apostles' doctrine. The early Church was laid upon the foundation of the prophets and Jesus Christ himself being the chief corner stone. God can only move in the Church which preaches sound doctrine.

Paul admonished the Church of Galatia that even if he or an angel from heaven should preach to them a different gospel from the one that he preached to them, such a person should be accursed or be counted to hell.

In breaking bread, the Church remembers the death of our Lord Jesus Christ, its founder; in praying and fellowshipping together, the Church continues in unity. Yes, the Church of Jesus Christ experienced signs and wonders – in the early Church fear came upon every soul because of what was happening among the brethren.

Our God is the God who comes by fire and signs and wonders. Signs and wonders are available to a sanctified and purified Church. When the Church is purified, no satanic force can conquer it. Prophetic utterances will be common among the believers whenever they meet, and fear will come upon every soul.

In Eph. 5:26-27, we read, "That he might sanctify and cleanse it with the washing of water by the word. That he might present it to himself a glorious Church, not having spot or wrinkle or any such thing: but it should be holy without blemish." And the twenty fifth verse of Ephesian chapter five says, "Husbands, love your wives as Christ loved the Church and gave himself for it." No prophet prophesied of the birth of the Church except Jesus himself. Almost every prophet spoke of the coming of Jesus but not of building of the Church. The Church is solely for Jesus himself.

A great many bishops, apostles, prophets and pastors have taken the place of Jesus. Whenever you ask them, "How was Church Sunday service?" You would hear them say that, "At my Church, the service was okay on Sunday." I marvel because no clergy owns the Church; for the Church belong to Jesus himself. When you say, "my Church," then you are taking the place of God. To exalt yourself higher than God or Jesus, is wrong. You may have the financial muscles and resources to construct Church buildings, but that does not mean you that you own the Church. Jesus does.

Jesus died so that the Church could be born. He told Peter that, "Upon this rock I will build my Church and no gates of hell shall prevail against it." Without his death, burial, resurrection, ascension and outpouring the Holy Ghost there would not have been the birth of the Church. Jesus, now in heaven, still loves the Church. No wander he prays for the Church as the High Priest. Jesus loves the sanctified Church. In heaven above, he prays for the Church below.

Jesus has ushered a glorious Church, not having spot or wrinkle or any such thing. This is the Church that shall see signs and wonders and it is a balanced Church with a lot of manifestations. In Mark16:17-18, we read, "And these signs shall follow them that believe: In my name shall they cast out devils; they shall speak with new tongues. They shall also take up serpents; and if they drink any deadly thing it shall not hurt them. They shall lay hands on the sick and they shall recover. "Believers have been given these commissions above all satanic forces.

I have visited Churches that command bigger following and what surprises me most is that I don't see the casting out of demons in some few members of the congregation. Although the Church itself is a holy and glorious Church, not all who enter in it is holy. Some are sinners who need repentance, some are with challenges and many problems that need to be sorted out and some with demons to be cast out in the name of Jesus.

A healthy and a balanced Church is a Church of signs and wonders. People are filled with the Holy Ghost, demons are cast out, saints share everything in common, the Word of God is being preached in truth, people are being baptized and prophetic utterances are being heard.

Men of God who were Used in Prophetic Utterances

In Daniel 3:16-1, we read that, "Shadrack, Mishack and Abednego answered and said to the king, O Nebuchadnezer, we are not careful to answer thee in this matter. If be so, our God whom we serve is able to deliver us out of thine hand, O king. But if not, be it known unto thee we will not serve thy gods nor worship the golden image which thou hast set up." Shadreck, Mishack and Abednego refused to worship the golden image. They spoke prophetic word of declaration.

In Luke 4:8, we read, "And Jesus answered and said unto him, get thee behind me Satan; for it is written thou shall worship the Lord thy God and him only shalt thou serve." Anyone who worships anything other than God indulges in idolatry. The prophetic word of declaration of Shadrack, Misheck and Abednego, namely, that "…if be so our God whom we serve is able to deliver us out of thine hand, O king," speaks to this prophetic utterance.

Despite that, Nebuchadnezzar's anger rose up and he commanded that the furnace be heated seven times more. However, the three Hebrew gentlemen spoke prophetically. As they were being thrown into the furnace, God quenched the Babylonian inferno.

In Jonah 2:1-4, we find, thus:

> Then prayed unto the Lord his God out of the fish s belly. and said, I cried by reason of mine affliction unto the Lord and he heard me; out of the belly of hell cried I, and thou heardest my voice. For thou hadst cast me into the deep, in the midst of the seas; and floods compassed me about; all thy billows and thy waves passed over me, then I said, I am casted out of thy sight. Yet, I look again toward thy holy temple.

This was a prophetic prayer of Jonah, prayed whilst swallowed in the fish belly. The whale took Jonah into the deep. The deep speaks of the underground world or hades. Jesus mentioned Jonah in Mathew 12:40: "For as Jonas was three days and three nights in the whale's belly, so shall the son of man be three days and three knights in heart of the earth." The whale took Jonah into the bottomless pit and Jonah nearly felt the heat of hades and started repenting. Jesus, when he died, straight went to the underworld. By then hell or Gehenna was an adjoining to paradise. No wonder, Jesus had to transfer paradise from the underworld to the third heavens. "When he ascended up, he led captivity captive and gave gifts unto men," (Eph. 4:8). When Paul was beaten half dead in Lystra, he was caught up into paradise in the third heaven (see 2 Cor. 12:1-4).

As noted in Jonah 2: 2,4, Jonah cried in the belly of the whale. This was a prophetic prayer of Jonah when he was inside the belly. After repenting, he saw himself in the Temple at Jerusalem worshiping, exalting God. The prayer of Jonah was prophetic, and after three days and three nights, the whale spilled out or vomited Jonah onto the land and Jonah went straight to Nineveh to preach the gospel.

The late president F.T.J Chiluba ushered a prophetic word of declaration when he said Zambia should remain a Christian Nation in the preamble to the 1996 Zambian Constitution. He went on to appointing Peter Chitala as Minister of Religious Affairs and Vendors Desk. In 2015, President Edgar C. Lungu continued to propagate that Zambia should still remain a Christian Nation. He went on to declaring 18th of October as a National Day of Prayers and Fasting, making it a public holiday. President Lungu went on to appoint Honourable Godfridah Sumaili as Religious Minister and National Guidance.

A temple is under construction that is called National House of Prayers. What the late president

Chiluba spoke was a prophetic word of declaration that Zambia should remain a Christian Nation and it is being fulfilled right in our midst. In God's will, you can utter prophetic word of utterances through prayer, teaching and preaching of the gospel.

4 | A PRAYERFUL CHURCH

What is Prayer?

Prayer is human being's communion with God. It is the highest expression of man's religious nature. A true Church of God should be a Church that prays. Prayer is the centre of every activity that involves God. As the Church prays, it will always invite God in its midst.

In Acts 2:1-4 and 42, we read:

> And when the Day of Pentecost was fully come, they were all in one accord in one place and suddenly there came a sound from heaven as of a rushing mighty wind and filled all the house where they were sitting. And there appeared unto them cloven tongues as of fire and it sat upon each of them. And they were filled with the Holy Ghost and began to speak

> with other tongues as the spirit gave them utterances.... And they continued steadfastly in the apostles' doctrine and fellowship and the breaking of bread and in prayers.

The early Church was in one accord among all the saints. It was a Church of prayer, and it birthed the Day of Pentecost. The disciples were in prayer and that was one of the reasons why the Holy Ghost came upon them. They had created the atmosphere for that to happen. It is the Holy Ghost that gave them boldness, and people saw the apostles coming out of the upper room fearlessly.

Prayer generates power, strength and ability to perform. As they came out of the upper room, they started teaching and preaching the gospel of Jesus Christ. The Holy Ghost enabled them to start preaching and teaching in different languages of the world. Those who witnessed Day of Pentecost were amazed and marveled saying one to another, "Behold, are they not all these which speak Galileans? And how hear we every man in our own tongue wherein we were born?" Each apostle spoke a new language he had never spoken before. It could be that Peter spoke Parthian, James Medes, John Elimites, Andrew Mesopotamian, Philip Cappadocian, or Bartholomiel Pontus, the Asian language. The likes of Thomas, the ex-doubter probably spoke Phrygian and the likes of Levy could have spoken the language of the Pamphylians, and the list is the endless. All that happened as they waited and energized themselves through prayer.

In Mark 11:15-17, we read:

> And they came to Jerusalem; and Jesus went to the temple and began to cast out them that sold and brought in the temple and overthrew the tables of money changers and the seats of them that sold doves and would not suffer that any should carry vessel through the temple. And he taught saying unto them, is it not written, my house shall be called of all nations the house of prayer? But you have made it a den of thieves.

Surely, Jesus was not happy to see people trading inside the temple. The Jews took the temple as a trading zone. In the beginning of Jesus' ministry, he wiped out those who were trading in the temple. And close to the end of his ministry, he also wiped them who were selling in the temple of God. This tells us that the temple had become a usual place for trading. The High Priest Cephas took advantage of this and allowed more people to trade in the temple – because that way he could collect taxes and make profit. Jesus could not wait, he had to whip all of them who were trading in the temple. He warned them and rebuked them for turning God's temple into a den of thieves. The Church should always pray to worship God in truth and in spirit. A temple at Jerusalem was a sacred place, and it was to be a house of prayer.

After the outpouring of the Holy Ghost, more than two thousand years ago, there have been great rising in Churches and their focus on prayers, communion with God. The success of every Bishop, pastor, prophet and evangelist is to commune with God. The same applies to believers. 1 Thessalonian 5:17 commands the Church to "Pray without ceasing." Philippians 4:6, urges the Church to "Be careful for nothing; but in everything it is by prayer and supplication with thanksgiving, let your request be made known unto God." Prayer lifts the Church to higher heights and prayer also puts the Church under the shadow of the Almighty God.

Meditation

The combined Bible Dictionary states that to meditate is to contemplate or think. It can also be to ponder over and think on God. The Church should meditate on the Word of God. It is the duty of Bishops, pastors, prophets and evangelists to meditate on the Word of God, if they are to see good success.

In Joshua 1:8, we read, "This book of the law shall not depart out of thy mouth; but thou shalt meditate therein day and night, that thou mayest observed to do according to all that is written there in; for then thou shalt make thy way prosperous and thou shall have good success."

Meditation brings good results. It is through meditation that God can inspire us. Bishop David O Oyedepo in his book, *Anointed for a Breakthrough*, writes that by inspiration, Jacob the son of Isaac, was like a university graduate, for he came up with a mixture of chemicals. He took the outer layers of the chestnut, green poplar and hazel trees and mixed them and formed a veterinary medicine for cattle, sheep, ram and oxen. He put the mixtures in the drinking gutters, and when the animals came and drank in the water that was full of the chemicals, during breeding, they produced ring streaked, specked and spotted animals which Laban, his father-in-law, did not want. Jacob capitalized on this trick and became very rich in animal husbandry.

Similarly, by inspiration, Joseph the son of Jacob was like a holder of a degree in Agricultural Economics and Construction. He preserved food in silos and barns for seven years without rotting. There was seven years of bumper harvest in Egypt and another seven years of famine throughout the world. When Joseph interpreted the dream to Pharaoh, Joseph got promoted, and became second in command and responsible for anything concerning food storage and preserving. All this happened through meditation.

God inspires us through meditation.

The Bible is the best guide for meditation. The saints of God must study Bible verses and meditate on them. As a result, they will get inspiration from God. Somebody told me that if you start studying the Bible and meditate on the verses and chapters, you shall be great in the Word, because the Bible is the Word of God. The entire Bible is inspired of God. It contains science, technology, history, geography, statistics, psychology, intelligence, politics, and so on. The Bible is the best book of moral law; some of the criminal/penal law codifications were derived from the Ten Commandments.

Psalms 1:1-3 reads: "Blessed is the man that walketh not in the counsel of ungodly, nor standeth in the way of sinners, nor sitteth in the seat of the scornful. But his delight is in the law of the Lord, and in his law doth he meditates day and night. He shall be like a tree planted by the rivers of water, that bringeth forth his fruit in his season; his leaf shall not wither; and whatsoever he does shall prosper."

Christians who dedicate themselves to the things of God and seek him diligently, thinking all about him, pondering their thoughts on him, are blessed. They shall be like trees planted by the rivers of water.

In Acts 17:10-11, we read, "And the brethren immediately sent away Paul and Silas by night into Berea, who coming thither went into the synagogue of the Jews. These were more noble than those in Thessalonica, in that they received the word with readiness of mind and searched the scriptures daily, whether those things were so."

The people of Berea were expounders and meditators of God's word, and they received the Word with readiness of mind and Paul and Silas has less difficulty explaining the Word to them than to the Thessalonians.

On this point, I will reproduce the following from one of the greatest teachers of our time:

> Let me reiterate a secret to all preachers and teachers out there. Preaching is the least means of influencing people. Teaching is the best means of influencing people. Preaching has several flaws, including: The preacher cannot impart more than they know; preaching focuses only on one perspective, the preacher's; there is no way of correcting error in preaching (if the message or doctrine is erroneous, everyone flows with it, sadly); it shrinks creativity, listeners can't think beyond what they heard; and preaching is mostly directed at the heart, it fails to renew the mind, and so on.
>
> Teaching, on the other hand, does the following: It expands learning (through research); both the teacher and the student grow - they are able to probe issues further; there is little room for one-sided perspective, students can raise questions and object to what is not doctrinally correct; teaching renews the mind; teaching warrants creativity - that's why in the world, students have gone on innovating and creating new things; knowledge expands and is protected through teaching it from generation to generation, and so on.
>
> Consider all founders of great religions, they are all great teachers. Then consider Jesus' final injunction: "Go therefore and make disciples of all the nations, baptizing them in the name of the Father and of the Son and of the Holy Spirit, teaching them to observe all things that I have commanded you; and lo, I

am with you always, even to the end of the age. Amen."

You make converts by preaching; but you make disciples by teaching. Preach to people who are not believers, but teach believers. Or structure your sermons to be 90% teaching, and only 10% preaching.[1]

Men and Women of God Who Brought Good Result through Prayer and Meditations

1 Samuel 1:12-17 records:

> And it came to pass, as she continued praying before the Lord, that Eli marked her mouth, now Hannah, she spake in her heart; only her lips moved, but her voice was not heard: Therefore, Eli thought she had been drunken, and Eli said unto her, how long wilt thou be drunken? Put away thy wine from thee. And Hannah answered and said, no my Lord, I am a woman of a sorrowful spirit: I have poured out my spirit before the Lord. Count not thine hand maid for a daughter of belial; for out of the abundance of my complaint and grief I have spoken hitherto. Then Eli answered and said, go in peace and the God of Israel grant thee thy petition that thou hast asked of him.

Hannah was the first wife of Elkanah and Penninah was his second wife. Even though Hannah was

---

[1] Charles Mwewa, Facebook Posting of May 24th, 2020.

barren, her husband loved her and Penninah used to mock her because she had ten sons besides her daughters. In Shiloh, Hannah prayed and petitioned God over her barrenness until she entered into travailing prayer. All her inner being sobbed before God. Eli thought that she was drunk. But Hannah replied and said, "No, my Lord, I am a woman of sorrowful spirit; I have drunken neither wine nor strong drink, but I have poured my soul before the Lord." Eli was convinced and said, "Go in peace and the God of Israel grant you, your petition that you have asked him."

Hannah's prayer was characterized by petition and meditation. We know this because the Scripture says, "...for only her lips moved." Eli thought that Hannah was drunk with wine. Hannah did not only bare Samuel as the only son but she also had other children after that prayer. There is power in prayer and meditation.

2kings 4:33-37 records:

> He went therefore and shut the door upon them twain and prayed unto the Lord. And he went up and laid upon the child and put his mouth upon his mouth and his eyes upon his eyes and his hands upon his hands and stretched himself upon the child; and the child waxed warm, then he returned and walked in the house to and fro; and went up and stretched himself upon him; and the child sneezed seven times and opened his eyes. And he called Gehazi and said, call this

> Shunammite. So, he called her and went in and fell at his feet and bowed herself to the ground and took up her son and went out.

Only Elisha and the dead child were locked up in the upper chamber. Elisha prayed to God in the room while the dead boy was laid on the bed of the man of God. After a series of prayers, Elisha went up and laid upon the dead child and he faced his mouth upon the mouth, his eyes upon his eyes and his hands upon his hands and stretched upon the dead boy.

The first time Elisha laid upon the dead body; the boy waxed warm. Elisha walked up from the bed moving to and from, in the house uttering prayers. Elisha went again and laid on the dead boy and the boy sneezed seven times and opened his eyes and resurrected. The movements Elisha was making in the chamber and the series of prayers he uttered, constituted meditation. His meditations were characterized by thanksgiving type of prayer and surrendering the dead boy in the hands of its Creator and the child was restored and came back to life.

The miracle Elijah did to the son of a widow of Zarephath – stretching himself upon the child three times and crying unto the Lord, resurrected the boy to life, (See I Kings 17:19-22). Point to note is that Elijah did this miracle in a foreign land and Elisha, did his in Israel. Elijah was a prophet of judgment and he prayed to God with a commanding voice and said, "O, Lord my God, hast thou also brought evil upon the widow with whom I sojourn, by slaying her son?"

Another point to observe is that both Elijah and Elisha laid on male children and not female children. In these passages of scriptures, God is a God who respects gender. Elijah and Elisha slept on top of the male dead bodies and not on female dead bodies. When Peter raised Dorcas to life, he did not stretch himself upon her or slept on top of her. Peter kneeled down and prayed; and turning to the dead he said, "Tabitha [Dorcas], arise," and she opened her eyes (see Acts 9:40). True prophets of God will respect gender and will not abuse women or men.

In the dispensation of the Holy Ghost or the Church Age, we have been admonished to lay hands, either on the sick, dead or those who are seeking for blessings and salvation, respectively. 1 Timothy 4:14, we read, "Neglect not the gift that is in therewith was given thee by prophecy, with the laying on the hands of the presbytery."

We also further note that the dead can be raised through prayer and meditation. The sick can be healed through prayers and meditation. Blessings can come through prayer and meditation and demons possessed people can be delivered through prayer and meditation.

Prayer and Fasting

Fasting is abstaining from any food. Just abstaining from any food but without praying, is not enough. A certain preacher said that abstaining from any food and failure to pray it is just hunger strike. In Mathew 6:16-18, we are read: "Moreover when you fast, be not as hypocrites of sad countenance; for they disfigure their faces that they may appear unto men to fast. Verily, verily, I said unto you, they have their reward. But when you fast, anoint thine head and wash your face that thou appear not unto men to fast, but unto thy Father which is in secret; and thy Father which seeth in secret shall reward thee openly." In Isaiah 58:5-6, it is written, "Is it a fast that I have chosen, a day for a man to afflict his soul? Is it to bow down his head as bulrush and to spread sackcloth and ashes under him? Wilt thou call this a fast and an acceptable day to the Lord? Is not this the fast that I have chosen, to loosen the hands of the wicked, to undo the heavy burdens, to let the oppressed go free?"

Man is connected to this world by food. It was actually with food man was tempted in the Garden of Eden and he fell. Esau sold his birth right because of food. The Lord Jesus Christ was first tempted with food but he triumphed over the devil because of fasting and prayer. Jesus entered into fasting and prayer *full of the Holy Ghost* and came out in the *power of the Holy Ghost!* Mathew is telling us that we need not to be hypocrites, or be double standard people. Do not disclose to anyone that you are fasting except to the members of your local Church, or your closest friends. For you share something in common with members of your family.

It is important to wash yourself and put lotions or oil on your body when you are fasting before God. God is the only one who sees you and knows that you are fasting. Good News Bible translates Isaiah 58:5-6 as follows: "When you fast, you make yourself suffer; you bow your head low like a blade of grass and spread out sackcloth and ashes to lie on. Is that what you call fasting? Do you think I will be pleased with that? The kind of fasting I want is this: Remove the chains of oppression and the yoke of the injustice and let the oppressed go free." Mathew 17:21 renders it, "Albeit this kind goeth not out but by prayer and fasting."

In the Old Testament, when fasting, they used to put on ashes and sackclothes. Mordecai, in Shushan City, put on himself sackcloth and ashes, and cried in the street. Esther thought that Mordechai had become insane In the New Testament, we are admonished when fasting, to wash ourselves clean and look sharp.

You enter fasting and praying in order to seek God at a higher level. There are other challenges that do not need prayer, and others that need prayer only but also others that need both prayer and fasting. In fasting, you are saying that you are extending your hands to the Lord. And God will break down the chains of oppression when you fast. God will break the yoke of injustice when you are fast. As you fast, what have been challenges in your life shall be wiped away. When you seek God in his will, all the valleys and hills of your life shall be levelled!

Jesus said, "Come unto me ye all that labor and are heavy laden and I will give you rest." It is through fasting and prayer that this is possible. You may be oppressed, however through fasting and prayer, you shall be liberated in your life. If the Son, therefore, shall make you free, you shall be free indeed (see John 8:36)!

Five Principles of a Biblical Fasting[2]

1. There must be a need

A fasting engagement without a well-defined purpose is futile. You must from the outset define the motive behind your fasting assignment sometimes it is nicer to list down what you expect to achieve at the end of your fast. At the end of it, you can be rest assured of a victory in Jesus' name.

2. The need must be inspired by the Holy Spirit

Sometimes, it is wiser to make suitable programs, committing yourself to weekly or monthly prayers. These prayers and fasting are supernaturally activated.

---

[2] These are directly derived from *Prayer: All Prayer Makes All Things Possible*, by Charles Mwewa

God will honour any fasting that glorifies him. Especially in a very long fasting, the Holy Ghost must a deciding factor. This is because certain people go on fasting for certain reasons. Some for health and others as a result of religious myth!

3. The need inspired by the Holy Ghost must be done in love.

A fasting engagement without love is in vain. The fact that you are fasting doesn't mean that you have to resent your brother and your sister. During fasting, care must be taken to avoid unnecessary temptations to look down on those who do not fast. Let love compel us to fast. Let us fast in love.

4. Food Consumption

Certain people will consume everything that they budgeted for that particular day of fasting either the day before fasting or the day after. It has been encouraged that food which was meant for the day of fasting should be given to the poor or the money which could have bought food for that day be given to the needy. Then that fast will be done in line with the express will of God. This is what we may refer to as a hospitality aspect of fasting.

5. Prayer and fasting must be conducted in secret

We should not pose as though we are fasting or to show everyone that we are fasting.

Expected Result of a Successful Fasting

It is an act of humbling the body and soul, bringing forth light, accelerating healing, assuring God's presence, glorifying God, and ensuring that every prayer prayed has been answered.

Other results expected from fast are: Lifting up miseries; ensuring divine guidance; meeting of needs; keeping us health; bringing restorations and joy.

Fasting release God's favour and you become more sensitive to the Holy Ghost. Moreover, fasting brings understanding, and releases you into a dynamic ministry. You are assured of guidance for ministerial duties in fasting. In addition, fasting releases divine deliverance; is the will of God; and is rewarding.

A Church that prays, fasts, studies the Word of God, and meditates on the things of God, shall be strong. Fasting is the life line of the Church.

5 | HOLY GHOST FIRE

Holy Ghost Fire

In Acts, it is written, "But you shall receive power, after the Holy Ghost is come upon you; and you shall be my witness unto me both in Jerusalem and in all Judea and in Samaria and unto the uttermost part of the earth."[3] We read further:

> But this shall be a covenant that I will make with the house of Israel: After those days saith the Lord, I will put my law in their inward parts, and write in their hearts; and I will be their God and they shall be my people. And they shall teach no more every man his neighbour and every man his brother, saying know the Lord: For they shall know me, from the least of them unto the greatest of them,

[3] Acts 1:8

> saith know the Lord. For I will forgive their iniquity and remember their sins no more.[4]

No one received the Holy Ghost under the dispensation of the law. Receiving the Holy Ghost started on the Day of Pentecost and that is when the Church was born. The children of Israel recited the Ten Commandment by heart only. The law served as their school masters, and it pointed them to Jesus Christ.

In the Bible, we read:

> And the Lord spake unto Moses, saying, speak unto the children of Israel and bid them that they make fringes in their borders of their garments throughout their generations, and that they put upon the fringe of the borders a ribband of blue. And it shall be upon unto you for a fringe, that you may look upon it and remember all the Ten Commandments of the Lord and do them and that ye seek not after your own heart and your own eyes after which you use to go a whoring.[5]

The children of Israel were commanded to make tassels on their corners of their garments and put a blue cord on each tassel. The tassels served as reminders and each time they touched the tassels; they remembered the Ten Commandments (The Torah).

---

[4] Jeremiah 31:33-34

[5] Numbers 15:37-39

Jesus Christ was born toward the end of the dispensation of the law; he was also part of the dispensation of the law. Despite that, he is the author of the law; he wore garments that had tassels on the corners. The woman who suffered with an issue of blood for twelve years (who had cervical cancer), penetrated her hand on the border of Jesus Christ's garment in a crowded atmosphere. In Luke 8:44, we are reminded, thus, "She came behind him and touched the border of his garment; and immediately her issue of blood stanched."

The woman touched the core, the heart of the law. No wander power went off from Jesus' body. The woman was righteous despite the fact that she suffered with an issue of blood. Power went off from Jesus' body because righteous and righteousness attract. If at all she was a sinner even though she had touched Jesus, nothing would have happened at all. Remember there were many who touched Jesus but he did not feel any impact. Righteousness and sin are opposed to each other, just as a magnet cannot attract wood.

Jesus came not to destroy the law but to fulfill the law. Remember the moral law, that is the Ten Commandments, is still working even today. Jesus divides the Ten Commandments into two categories, thus: (1) Category number one, Mark 12: 29-30, "And Jesus answered him, the first of all the commandments is hear, O Israel, the Lord thy God is one Lord. And thou shall love the Lord thy God with all thy heart and with all thy soul and with all thy mind and with all thy strength; this is the first commandment; and (2) Category number two, Mark 12:31, "And the second is alike, namely, thou shall love thy neighbour as thyself. There is none other commandment greater than this."

Categories one and two are packaged in Exodus 20:1-17 which records the Ten Commandments. Ceremonial laws (moral laws other than the Ten Commandments) were pointing to Jesus, the image of good things to come. When Jesus died, the veil in the temple was torn apart, a symbol that there would be no more killing of lambs or goats, putting an end to sacrificial worship. Jesus Christ became the ultimate sacrificial lamb. Other examples, include Jesus the Passover lamb – embodied in the Feast of Trumpet and, thus, a type of unleavened bread. He is now the central figure concerning the ceremonial laws.

In additional to the Ten Commandments, sacrificial or ceremonial laws, Moses also penned 613 civil laws which Israel was to follow. In the civil law, Moses with the governance of Israel. Even today these laws must be followed when it comes to the governance of a country. In almost every country, people should follow these laws even today).[6]

Under the law, the children of Israel were to follow the laws. Symbolism is very prevalent in the moral laws, especially to do with the Holy Spirit, since he had not been poured on everyone then: The symbols of the Holy Spirit are a dove, water, anointing oil,

[6] Consider Roman 13:1

thunder, lightening, and fire. Despite the fact that the Holy Ghost was not yet poured in the dispensation of the law or in the Old Testament, Israel saw God appear as theophany: A **theophany** is a visible manifestation of God and we usually think of it as temporal in nature. As God is invisible to man, to make himself visible, he manifested himself in a physical form. Even though no one could see the Spirit of God, they saw the representation of God.

Since fire and dove are one of the symbols of the Holy Ghost, I will explain more on these: In Gen. 15:17-18, "And it came to pass, when the sun went down and it was dark, behold a smoking furnace and a burning lamp that passed between those pieces. On the same day the Lord made a covenant with Abraham, saying, unto thy seed I have given the land from the river of Egypt unto the great river Euphrates." In the Palestinian covenant, land was given to Abraham's seed. Abraham was given the land of Palestine, which would be passed on to his descendants, Israel. Abraham's seed, a single seed, is Jesus Christ. This Jesus Christ would repossess the Palestinian land which had been intruded on by foreign nations.

This will happen at the Battle of Armageddon, thereafter, he will rebuild the new temple which was destroyed in 70 A.D by the Romans. At this time, that area is where the Muslim's Mosque is built. When the new temple shall be built, Jesus will rule in the millennium and almost every believer will worship in or towards that place.

Jesus, as the seed of the woman, came and crushed the devil when he provided salvation to all mankind, when he died on the cross of calvary and shed blood for the whole world. Satan thought that he had defeated Jesus when Jesus died and thought that Jesus would not resurrect, but little did Satan know that on the third day, Jesus would be resurrected.

With the Palestinian covenant, land was ushered in to Abraham, when the Lord appeared unto him. He told him to take a heifer, an ewe and a ram of three years, dressed them and divided them into equal parts. He took the divided pieces of meats and put them equally, some to the left and some to the right and in between them he left a space. He took a turtle dove and a young pigeon and dressed them but he did not divide them; he took each of them and put one to the right where he put the meats and the other to the left and the same space was between those carcasses. Abraham was there waiting that God would come and make a covenant with him. The wild animals came trying to eat the meats but Abraham chased them away. During the night, Abraham fell asleep, and it was when God came in the form of a smoking furnace and burning lamp and passed between those pieces. That is how God made a covenant with Abraham, to his seed he gave him the land.

God came in the form of the Holy Spirit, a smoking furnace and a burning lamp. There is an English saying that, "There's no smoke without fire." The smoking furnace and burning lamp are the symbols of the Holy Spirit.

God appeared to Moses in a burning bush but the bush did not burn. God came with the message to go and deliver the children of Israel in Egypt. The burning bush was fire and the fire was the Holy Ghost (see Exodus 3:8).

When Jesus went into the Jordan River to be baptized by John the Baptist, Jesus saw the heaven opened and the Spirit of God descending like a dove and lightening upon him (see Mathew 3:16). That was God in the form of a dove and lightening. Remember Jesus was born under the dispensation of the law and came to usher in a new beginning, the dispensation of the Holy Ghost.

Despite that, in the Old Testament no-one received the baptism of the Holy Ghost. Israel saw tresses of the symbol of the Holy Ghost when God appeared in a form of a dove or fire, lightening, water (cloud) or earthquake. Jerbal Gideon saw God appear in a form of fire. It was the time when Israel was defeated by the Midianites – crops, cattle, sheep and oxen were looted. Whenever Israel disobeyed God's commandments, things did not go well for them. During the time when Judges ruled, people did what was good in their own eyes.[7]

God brought cycles of afflictions during those times when Israel had no kings to rule over them. God raised Gideon that he should go and conquer the Midianites and repossess all that they had looted from Israel. Before he could do that, Gideon wanted to

---

[7] See Judges 21:25

know the sign if under his leadership he would defeat the Midianite. God told Gideon to get meat, bake unleavened cakes and make soup. He took all these and put them on a rock and took a rod and pointed it straight where the meats, unleavened cakes and soup were. Then when he saw an angel coming, he burnt those sacrifices.

Sometimes God can appear in a form of an angel. Gideon was assured by an angel that he could overcome the Midianites and he went to the battle front and defeated them. Really, it was God in a form of fire. To Ezekiel, he appeared in a form of a man enveloped in fire.[8] God appeared to Moses in a cloud and in fire on Mount Sinai, and God spoke to him face to face in the tabernacle and revealed to him his back (partial glory) and not his face (full glory).[9]

These references to God's face and God's glory probably are metaphoric of the presence of God and could apply to many types of manifestations. God manifested himself in the sight of all Israel through thunder and lightning, a cloud, a voice of the trumpet, and smoke, fire and earthquakes.[10] He also showed his glory and sent fire from his presence in the sight of all Israel.[11]

---

[8] Ezekiel1:26-28

[9] Ex. 24:12-18, 33:9-11, 33:18-23

[10] Ex. 19:11-19, Deut. 5:4-5, 22-27

[11] Lev. 9:23-24; Lev. 10:1-2.

In the Old Testament, it was only God who used to appear in these forms: Fire, lightening, smoke, dove, clouds or water and these are all symbols of the Holy Ghost. Jeremiah and Ezekiel prophesied of the covenant that God would make with the house of Israel; that God would put his laws in their inward parts and write them in their hearts and he would be their God and they will be his people. And they should teach no more every man his neighbour and every man his brother saying, "Know the Lord." Jeremiah and his counterpart Ezekiel prophesied of the Holy Ghost fire which would be in the hearts of the believers. And they would not be reciting the laws any more, no more touching the borders of the garments to remember the laws and no more touching inside the pockets or at the corner of skirts in order to remember the laws because the Holy Spirit inside the believers would teach them. This is the Holy Ghost that is leading now in all the truth.

Joel prophesied of the Holy Ghost and he said that it would come to pass afterward that God would pour his spirit upon all flesh: and their sons and daughters would prophesy, their old men would dream dreams, their young men would see visions: And also, upon the servants and upon the hand maids in those days God would pour out his spirit.[12]

John the Baptist said, "I indeed baptize you with water unto repentance: but he that cometh after me is mightier than I, whose shoes I am not worthy to bear:

[12] See Joel 2:28-29

He shall baptize you with the Holy Ghost and fire.[13] In the fourteenth chapter of the Gospel of John, Jesus promised his disciples that he would return to them after his ascension in the form of the Holy Ghost, the comforter or the spirit of truth. Jesus referred to the promise as the rivers of living water flowing from believers: "He that believeth on me as the scripture hath said, out of his belly shall flow rivers of living water (but this spake he of the Holy Ghost, which was not yet given: because that Jesus was not yet glorified).[14]

Luke records Jesus' assurance to us that the Holy Ghost is a good gift from God and that he would gladly give it to us if we desire and seek it.[15] And he said:

> Ask and it shall be given you: seek and you shall find and knock and it shall be opened unto you. And he that seeketh findeth: to him who knocketh, it shall be opened. If a son shall ask bread of any of you that is a father, will he give him a stone? Or if he asks a fish, will for a fish give him a serpent? Or if he shall ask an egg, will he offer him a scorpion? If ye then, being evil, know how to give good gifts unto your children: How

---

13 Mathew 3:11

14 John 8:38:39

15 Luke11:9-13

> much more shall your heavenly father give
> the Holy Ghost to them that ask him?[16]

God desires all men to receive the gift of the Holy Spirit. All men what they need to do is to believe on God as the scriptures have said. The works of the Holy Ghost in the believers are imputation, sanctification, regeneration and purification.

Imputation

By imputation or to impute is a process where God declares a sinner to be righteous. It is a process where God removes the sins of someone and he forgets and that person becomes automatically righteous. I talked to someone on the bus that it is possible to forgive someone and forget and he answered me that a human being cannot forgive and cannot forget, surely God can forgive and forget. The Bible declares: "There is therefore now no condemnation to them which are in Christ, who walk not after the flesh but after the spirit."[17]

Paul was a creature whom they used to condemn even when God had forgiven his sins. They knew him as a murderer, and a persecutor of the Church but little did they know that God had forgiven his sins

[16] Matthew 7:7-11

[17] Roman 8:1

when the Lord appeared to him as a flash light on the road to Damascus. God imputed Paul's sins and God forgot. When God has imputed your sins, he has also forgotten.

Sanctification

Sanctification means to set apart. Under the Mosaic law, the priests and the Levites were set apart for a special service. The objects they used in the tabernacle were also sanctified and even days were set apart for special use. In the New Testament, it means to be made inwardly whole. The agent of this sanctification is the Holy Ghost.[18] It is the indwelling of Christ himself. Believers are referred to as saints.[19] To sanctify is to dedicate and make holy. Note the following verses on sanctification:

"And I will sanctify the tabernacle of the congregation and the alter and I will sanctify also both Aaron and his sons to minister to me in the priestly office."[20]

"For I am the Lord your God: ye shall be holy: for I am holy: neither shall ye defile yourselves with any

---

[18] Rom15:16

[19] Rom. 12:13

[20] Ex. 29:44

manner of creeping thing that creepeth upon the earth."[21]

"Sanctify them through thy faith: thy word is truth."[22]

The Holy Ghost teaches us the truth and that truth sanctifies us. You must sanctify the Lord in your hearts and be always ready to give an answer to every man that asks you by reason of hope that is in you, with meekness and fear. This subject was also discussed in Chapter Three of this book.

Regeneration

Regeneration is the change wrought in the thought, feeling and will of man in his relation to God and the world. The fact that God demanded obedience rather than sacrifice shows that God dealt with the heart of a man. The tension found in the morality of the Old Testament was resolved in the New Testament idea of regeneration, being born again. The Holy Ghost brings regenerations in our lives: "Therefore if a man be in Christ, he is a New creature: old things are passed away: behold, all things are become new."[23]

---

[21] Lev. 11:44

[22] John 17:17

[23] 2 Cor. 5:17

And "For this cause also thank we God, without ceasing, because when you received the Word of God which you heard of us, you received it not as word of men but as it is in truth, the Word of God which effectually worketh also in you that believe."[24]

The Word of God regenerated the believers in Thessalonica because they accepted the Word of God with faith. James says that faith without work is dead. The Word of God must be taken seriously before it can start to work in our souls. The Holy Ghost fire regenerates believers and moves them from one glory to glory.

Purification

Is the cleansing of the ceremonially unclean person. Cleanliness even now is considered desirable in the Bible land as elsewhere. But cleanliness is more than bodily cleanliness, it means acceptability before God. King Ahasuerus was disappointed by his wife. The queen was supposed to come and appear before the governors of the king and show her beauty during the feast but she failed to attend. That was a great disappointment before the king, the governors and the people at large. The king and members of the royal family sat together and decided that the king should terminate the marriage and look for virgins who would go into purifications after a season of

[24] 1 Thessalonian 2:13

beautifying themselves, then the king would come and choose one virgin to be the queen of Medes and Persia.

The virgins were to cleanse themselves, with costly oil, bedecked with costly ornaments and when that time came for the king to choose his wife, Esther a Jewess virgin found favor in the eyes of the king and she became the queen.

That is what the Holy Ghost does, it cleanses and purifies the body. Believers are purified by the agency of the Holy Ghost. The Word of God that we hear cleanses and purifies believers. It is like silver tried in the furnace of the earth and which is purified seven times. Twenty-four carat gold when it is melted, it glitters, brighter and more purified than before because all the impurities are removed. The Good News Bible says: "He gave himself for us to rescue us from all the wickedness and to make us pure people who belong to him alone and are eager to do good."[25] And again, "And every man that hath this hope in him purifieth himself, even as he is pure."[26] This work of the Holy Ghost fire is to purify believers as they keep on moving with Christ Jesus. All the impurities, quietly, quietly are being washed away.

[25] Titus 2:14

[26] 1 Peter 3:3

Receiving the Holy Ghost Fire

There has been a wrong teaching among some Church organizations about who gives the Holy Spirit. The Holy Spirit is God himself and nobody can give the Holy Spirit apart from God himself. Don't be deceived by the prophets, pastors, apostles and evangelists who preach that they can give believers the Holy Spirit by their own effort. God (Father) is the only one who can fill you with the Holy Spirit: "For there are three that bear record in heaven, the father, the word and the Holy Ghost and these are one."[27] These speak of one thing. The Father is the source of the Holy Ghost. God is a Spirit and they that worship him must worship him in truth and in spirit. The word is God himself, him being invisible made this world by only speaking the word. In the beginning was the Word, and the Word was with God. The word became flesh and dwelt among us. The Father, the Son and the Holy Ghost are not three personalities but one person. There would never be three personalities of God. God is the only Supreme Being, he doesn't know any other god besides him.[28] There are no three trinity in the Godhead. Those three are not three in numerical terms but they are three in their offices. God is the Father of all creations, he became the Son in redemption and is now the Holy Spirit in

---

[27] 1 John 5:7

[28] Isaiah 44:6

regeneration or in the Church Age: "And without controversy great is the mystery of godliness: God was manifested in the flesh, justified in the spirit, seen of angels, preach unto the gentiles, believed on the world and received up unto glory."[29]

God is a Spirit at some point he incarnated in human form. The Holy Spirit is God and overshadowed virgin Mary and she conceived. The Son, Jesus, was born and they called him Immanuel that means God is with us. Christ Jesus is the Son of God because the Holy Spirit, to be God, facilitated that he should be born through Mary. They are not two personalities here or three but one. God and Holy Spirit, in Greek *nehuma* or air, invisibly entered in the womb of Mary and she became pregnant. That baby Jesus was hundred percent full of the Holy Spirit equal to God, the invisible God. For the first time they saw God in a human form in Bethlehem of Judah when Jesus was Born. Christ Jesus had two dual natures; he was God and human. The Holy Spirit is God who became the Son in redemption. God thought for a man who could come and die for the whole world and there was no one, the blood of a human was needed but there was no one to take that position. So, God humbled himself and came in a human form. God being invisible or air saw that no one was able to redeem mankind, the blood of the lamb that the priest performed sins offering with could just push away the sins of Israel until the

[29] 1 Timothy 3:16

following year. So, there was a need for God to come and die himself for the world and to save mankind. The Holy Spirit, air, and word turned into a human being so that he would shed blood and save all humanities because of the mistakes of our first parents, Adam and Eve.

I acknowledge Jesus as the Son of God but not God the Son. In English, if you say, "God the son," it means that there is another God who is less equal to God the Father and it is tantamount to two or three persons of God and that is a heresy. God will never share his glory with anyone. He is the self-existence one and there would never be three people of Gods; that is impossible. The body of Christ Jesus was elevated when he died, resurrected and when he went up to heaven.[30] The Bible is clear on this:

> Wherefore God (which is equivalent to the Spirit, the Father, the source, the invisible and air) hath highly exalted him (Spirit, air, God has exalted the body of Christ Jesus) and given him the name which is above every name(God the invisible inside the body of Christ).At the name of Jesus every knee shall bow(there is no separation between God and Christ Jesus or the Holy Spirit and the body that brought salvation to humanities is one), of things in heaven (if Jesus is different from God or Holy Spirit, then he is above all thing in heaven and he became the God Almighty then there would

[30] See Philippians 2:9-11

> be confusion in heaven. It is the body of Christ Jesus where the father or the Holy Spirit, air and an invisible God that is inside and the one we shall see in human form will be Jesus, that is, God himself when he comes in the final judgment, for the Spirit or the air cannot judge. A judge is always a human being) and of things in earth (whatsoever we do in deed and in word do them in the name of the Lord Jesus)[31] and things under earth. And that the name of Jesus every knee should bow (they can never be three personalities of Gods, if there is God the Father then, he is bowing down to God the Son and that is impossible. Jesus is the very God who is one) and things under the earth. And every tongue should confess that Jesus is Lord, to the glory of God the Father.[32]

Jesus said that it was expedient for him to go to heaven so that the Holy Spirit or the comforter should come.[33] The Holy Spirit is one, anything other than two or more spirits that is of the devil. The Holy Spirit is Jesus himself, and no wonder he told them that he had to go in his physical body so that he would send the Holy Spirit to the believers. The same modes of operation: God in creation, Son in redemption and the Holy Ghost in regeneration. The same one God

---

31 Col 3:1

32 Ibid.

33 John 16:17

but different in operations. On the Day of Pentecost, for the first time, they received the Holy Ghost and he continued to be poured on believers. A human being cannot give you the Holy Spirit, only God or Jesus. The first sermon Peter preached on the Day of Pentecost climaxed and those who came to listen to him, they received the gift of the Holy Ghost:

> Therefore, let the all house of Israel know assuredly that God hath made the same Jesus whom you crucified, both Lord and Christ. Now when they heard this, they were pricked in their heart and said unto Peter and the rest of the apostles, men and brethren what shall we do? Then Peter said unto them repent and be baptized every one of you in the name of Jesus for the remission of sin and you shall receive the gift of the Holy Ghost. For the promise is unto you and to your children and to all that are afar off, even the Lord our God shall call.[34]

The apostles received the Holy Ghost with the initial evidence of speaking in other tongues or languages. One spoke the language of the Parthians, another of the Medes and the other of the Elamites and so on. The crowd that came to hear the Word of God on the Day of Pentecost was amazed and said, "Behold are

[34] Acts 2:36-39

not all these speak Galilean? And how hear we every man in our own tongue, where in we were born?"[35]

Another evidence that a believer has received the gift of the Holy Ghost is to speak with stammering lips as prophesied by Isaiah. It is also called tongue of angels, which no one understands, including the speaker himself and the hearer unless there is someone who has the gift of interpreting. A believer starts with stammering, as he continues to speak it, and finally he will be speaking the unknown tongue fluently. In the law it is written, "With men of other tongues and other lips will I speak unto this people,"[36] and "Yet for all that will they not hear me saith the Lord."[37]

One advantage of speaking in an unknown tongue is to edify yourself but not the Church. Jude encourages the saints to be praying in the Holy Ghost: "But ye beloved, building up yourselves on your most holy faith, praying in the Holy Ghost."[38] Other advantages of praying in unknown tongues are for believers to grow in the faith; as a sign not to them, but to them that believe not.[39] A non-believer is very much surprised to hear someone speaking in

---

[35] Acts 2:7-8

[36] Isaiah 28:11

[37] See 1 Cor. 14:21

[38] See Jude 20

[39] 1 Cor. 14:22

unknown tongue and will always want to see to it that he receives the gift of the Holy Ghost provided that he believes and repents of his sins.
Speaking in unknown tongue is even better when there is someone who has the gift of interpretation and this is equal to the task with the one who can teach and preach the Word of God. The Bible says: "If any man speaks in an unknown tongue, let it by two or at most by three and that by course: and let one interpret."[40]

There has been a great controversy among Church organizations over the doctrine of speaking in unknown tongues. Some believe that not every believer can receive the gift of speaking in an unknown tongue and others still believe that it is possible that every believer can speak in tongues provided that he has fully repented. Another verse of scripture says, "Do they all have the gift of healing? Do all speak with tongues? Do all interpret? But covet earnestly the best gifts and yet shew unto you a more excellent way."[41] In another place it is written: "Wherefore brethren, covet to prophesy and forbid not to speak with tongues. Let all things be done decently and in order."[42]Professor and pastor of New Life Tabernacle, United Pentecostal Church International, David K Benard in his book, *Spiritual*

---

[40] 1 Cor. 14:27

[41] 1 Cor. 12:30-31

[42] 1 Cor. 14:39-40

Gifts, indicates that a believer must receive the Holy Spirit with the initial evidence of speaking in unknown tongue at some point but that does not mean that he can continue speaking it all the time, the fact that he spoke it for the first time was enough. A true Church is the Church that is full of the Holy Ghost fire, believers speak in tongues, the word of encouragement is heard, and prophesy and signs and wonders happen among the saints. Such is a balanced Church, full of the unction of the Holy Ghost fire. It is not just enough to say, "Believe in the name of Jesus Christ," true salvation includes repentance, baptism in the name of Jesus and receiving the gift of the Holy Ghost.

ABOUT THE AUTHOR

Pastor Charles Chibwe is the founder and Pastor of the New Heaven Church Ministries. He has been in Ministries for some years. He is a charismatic preacher, teacher and mentor and a conference guest speaker whom the Lord has raised. After much studying the holy book (Bible), God has raised him to be spiritual books and sermons writer. Pastor Chibwe lives in Lusaka Zambia, South Central Africa. Pastor Chibwe s wife Abigail and their children, Zachariah, Cynthia and Destiny. For more information, contact him at: Cell: +260 (095) 369-4007; Email: chibwecharles881@gmail.com

INDEX

www.ingramcontent.com/pod-product-compliance
Lightning Source LLC
LaVergne TN
LVHW010116170826
845678LV00012B/2437

* 9 7 8 1 9 8 8 2 5 1 2 2 6 *